HEAVENLY WORSHIP
from the Book of
REVELATION

Esther Phillips-Dwyer

ISBN: 978-0-9982479-0-8 (sc)
ISBN: 978-0-9982479-1-5 (e)

Lulu Publishing Services rev. date: 05/18/2017

Dedication

This book is lovingly dedicated to:

- My Lord and Savior, Jesus Christ, who freely and unconditionally loves us.
- In fond memory of my greatly loved and missed son, Eddie, who has joined my dear parents, in the presence of our Lord.
- My beloved family, whom I love and appreciate very much.

CONTENTS

ACKNOWLEDGEMENTS

I am sincerely grateful firstly to My Lord and Savior, Jesus Christ, who gave me the honor of writing this book, His book. I thank God for my late, kind, loved, and loving, dear son, Eddie, who we miss greatly, and for his loving and devoted siblings, my precious children Michael, Matthew, Aaron, Jeremiah, and Elizabeth. I thank God for keeping us together as a family, and allowing us to encourage, pray for, assist, and support each other. Special thanks to my daughter, Elizabeth, who drew the wings full of eyes (Revelation 4:6-8), for the book's cover.

I am also deeply grateful to my late, dearly beloved, kind, caring, and loving Mom and Dad, who showed many the way to salvation, in Jesus Christ alone. In addition, they taught me how to pray, and sing hymns of worship to our Lord, as a young child. They also prayed for us unceasingly and supported us in every way they could.

I am also thankful to my dear siblings, Evans; my late kind and giving sister, Lynette; Annette; Judith; Audrey; Elton; Marleen; Peter; Patricia; Wendy and Paula; who prayed for us, and assisted us, especially during Eddie's illness and passing. Special thanks to my sisters Judith Bingham, MSN, RN; The Honorable Paula Wordsworth; LTC Marleen Phillips, Esq.; Patricia Phillips-Hutchinson; The Honorable Wendy Phillips; Reverend Dr. Audrey Jackman, and our brother Pastor Dr. Elton Phillips, for their special kindness and fervent support during those very trying experiences.

Further, I am deeply grateful to my Bishop and Pastor, T. D. Jakes, whose prayer, teaching, and ministry team, all so greatly helped us in so many ways. I am also grateful to my Lord for the anointed music by Terry MacAlmon, and his "Live Worship" CD, which helped me make it through some very tumultuous times.

Moreover, these songs of worship ushered me into the direct presence of my Lord. It was there that I found comfort from my Lord, and from reading about heavenly worship from the Book of Revelation, especially from chapters four and five. Thus, resulted in me becoming, a Heavenly Worshipper from the Book of Revelation.

I thank you all and dedicate this book to you, and to the many other dear loved ones who have helped us, prayed for us, and encouraged us. You, altogether with our Lord, played a vital part in saving our lives, and helped us get through some of the most difficult, and challenging times of our lives. As a result, I give my Lord all the glory for all the great things He has done. Not only did He protect, provide, and keep us but He also allowed you to positively impact our lives. While teaching me to worship Him from the Book of Revelation.

FOREWORD

I was convicted by our Lord to write this book for His purpose. I delayed and passively resisted as I felt inadequate. Our Lord showed me that it was not about me, but all about Him and His will. Accordingly, I was honored to be chosen for this purpose. Yet, I delayed, but wrote down what God delivered to me. Finally, I obeyed and began attempting to get this book published. As a result, "all hell broke loose". Amidst all the other troubles, my eldest son Eddie, who was a healthy 27-year-old, and who worked faithfully at his job for nearly 10 years, was diagnosed with stage 4 colon cancer. My family and I felt as if we were hit by a "ton of bricks". His struggle lasted 3 years. Throughout this ordeal, Eddie fought the best fight that he could while running the race with vigor and faith.

Mercifully, our loving and gracious Lord allowed Eddie to comfort, console, and reach thousands of dear ones with a message of hope, encouragement, and God's saving grace. Many of those that he inspired were also struggling with cancer or had family members who were dealing with the same. My son could say as the Apostle Paul, "I have fought the good fight, I have finished the race, I have kept the faith. Finally, there is laid up for me the crown of righteousness, which the Lord, the righteous Judge, will give to me on that Day, and not to me only but also to all who have loved His appearing." (2 Timothy 4:7-8).

Trouble can come to keep us in a state of confusion and to keep us from fulfilling our purpose. During these difficult times we must depend more on our Lord. He will see us through, and we will "understand it better by and by." Therefore, do not lose track of your purpose. Don't be discouraged or quit doing good deeds, because God has assured us that He will reward us at the right time. God will see us through. Stay on the path to success even when it gets rough. Say like Job, "though He slay me, yet will I trust Him...." (Job 13:15). Even though, our Holy Heavenly Father is not slaying us, but is perfecting us for His glory.

During the three years that Eddie was diagnosed with cancer, he accomplished more for the Lord, with greater intensity than I saw throughout his 27 years of not having cancer. His faith in God grew stronger as he demonstrated God's abundant love and kindness to many. His life reminded many of his co-workers of God's love. They stated that he was too kind for this world. Did he have faults and committed sins? Yes, he did, but thanks to God they were covered by the blood of Jesus. He was forgiven. Eddie was compassionate, giving and loved all.

Graciously, he freely shared the love of God, and his faith in God's healing power was strong. Yet, it pleased the Lord to take him without healing him from cancer. While he was on this earth, cancer laid a claim on his body, but now as he is with his Lord in heaven, cancer's claim is no longer valid. He was made whole in heaven. Eddie is dwelling with the Lord and his Savior, Jesus Christ forever and ever. Thus, as David said he cannot come to us, but one day we will go to him in heaven. There we will join Eddie in eternal heavenly worship of our Lord God Almighty, and the Lamb of God, Jesus Christ, our Blessed Redeemer.

TRUE HEAVENLYWORSHIP

The Book of Revelation is mainly considered a book of Bible prophecies in which many end-time events are revealed. However, the Book of Revelation is also a book which gives us glimpses of true heavenly worship around the throne of our Lord God Almighty, and before the Lamb, our Lord and Savior, Jesus Christ. Likewise, for us to experience what true heavenly worship is while we are on earth, we must first accept Jesus Christ as our Lord and Savior.

I thought that I knew what worship was about. However, as trials came, I realized that praising our Lord in the outer court was not enough. The outer court is similar to the outer court of the temple that Solomon built in which the people would gather. The High Priest would go into the Holy of Holies or the inner sanctuary, to meet with God once a year, on the Day of Atonement. There he would atone for his own sins, and if he lived, then for the sins of the people.

Thank God that we no longer require a High Priest to atone for us because of Jesus' atoning sacrifice for us on the cross. Rather, we can boldly enter into the presence of our Lord. Further, in God's direct presence, or in the inner sanctuary is where we would like to be. As we, "…the true worshippers will worship the Father in spirit and in truth; for the Father is seeking such to worship Him. 'God is a spirit; and those who worship Him must worship in spirit

1

and truth.' " (John 4:23-24).

Before we engage in heavenly worship, we should confess our sins to the Lord, for as David stated in Psalm 51:17, that God would not despise a broken and contrite heart. Engaging in heavenly worship requires us acknowledging our nothingness, and the all- encompassing nature of our Lord. That is recognizing that our Lord God Almighty is omnipotent, omniscient, and omnipresent. God in the person of His son, our Lord and Savior Jesus Christ, who is the King of kings and Lord of lords, humbled himself to die in our place. As a result, we cannot help but love and adore Him. When we worship our Lord with a broken and contrite spirit, all barriers which could keep us from entering the inner sanctuary are removed.

Sometimes during this time alone with my Lord, I would say Bible verses, and would sing songs of praise and worship. I do this in my quiet place, or while laying on the floor. I would also praise and glorify my Lord for He alone is worthy. During this period of worship, I would thank God for whom He is to us. I would also tell my Lord how much I love Him. Often times, I would then just wait quietly on my Lord. So direct is the connection with heaven that I would not want to be disturbed and would be blessed as God would speak back to my soul. All animals praise God, (Psalms 148:7, 10), and so should we. Accordingly, this book is intended to share these concepts, show how they occur in the Book of Revelation, and how they can occur in our lives. "Let everything that has breadth **praise the LORD. Praise the LORD!" (Psalm 150:6).**

I want everyone to worship God! I want us to fulfill our inner desire to be one with God. This means that we need to make Jesus Christ our Lord. We need to have His Holy Spirit, who is an equal part of the Trinity (which is comprised of The Father, Our Lord God Almighty; The Son, Jesus Christ, our Lord and Savior; and

2

The Blessed Holy Spirit, who dwells within us from the moment we are saved) dwelling within us. God's Blessed Holy Spirit is also called the Holy Ghost or our Comforter. When we are saved, the Holy Spirit is within us, directing us throughout our lives, and as we worship our Lord in the beauty of holiness.

People go to church looking for that closeness to God and many never find it. It is sad and heartbreaking to go to church week after week and see so many hungry souls looking for fulfillment, and looking for a closer relationship with God, and not finding it. Their souls cry out for rescue from trouble, danger, and discouragement. Sad to say, they come to church burdened, and may feel that joining in on the rituals of religion can be a substitute for the need to be saved.

As a result, they go home empty, unfulfilled, and even more burdened. They come back the next week for their one-hour treatment, but in the long-run it does not work. The burdens always get too heavy, and their euphoria only lasts for so long. They need to be told that they must be saved, and that the Holy Spirit must direct their lives. In order for the Blessed Holy Spirit to move them and direct them, they have to be saved, and need to be told how to do so.

They are hungry and crying out, and are not being fed. The first step is to be saved, which is to accept, believe in, and confess Jesus Christ as their risen Lord and Savior. "Nor is there salvation in any other, for there is no other name under heaven given among men by which we must be saved." (Acts 4:12). Additionally, in verse 10-11 of the same chapter, we are told that the name through which we get salvation is "Jesus Christ", who has become the chief cornerstone. (Also see the ABCs of God's Salvation Plan).

Some pastors can admit that they do not know how to lead someone to Christ. This is God's great commission which Jesus Christ, our Lord gave to us: to go into all the world and preach the

3

good news of salvation in Jesus Christ alone. Yes, there is a spiritual hunger that needs to be filled. The pastor, the staff, and the church all share a responsibility as to where that seeking soul will spend eternity. We need to make sure that souls do not leave the church in the same state that they entered; **they need to be saved and transformed.** This requires having their minds renewed. (Romans 12:1-2).

THE STRUGGLE TO BE A WORSHIPPER

Every resident of heaven will worship our Lord God Almighty and Jesus Christ, the Lamb of God, with heavenly worship throughout eternity. Therefore, let us begin to worship God with heavenly worship while we are on earth. Doing so, as we wait for that day in heaven when we will fall before our Lord's holy presence. In heaven, we will continuously worship our Lord. However, while we live on earth, our flesh wars against our spirit. The spirit may be willing to worship our Creator, but at times our flesh is weak.

Even though, God created us to worship Him, we can sadly admit that worship is not always easy for us. Surely, there are times when we have to talk ourselves into worshipping our Lord. During these times, we must battle against our flesh, and can present "sacrifices of praise" unto our God. As we remember that our Lord sent His beloved Son, Jesus Christ, to die on the cross for our sins.

As a result, we should also repent for our unwillingness to worship. After which, our thanksgiving and praise would naturally flow and change over into worship. At this time, we are worshipping God in our bodies and souls which are His. This is when we do not just enter into God's gates and His courts. Rather, we enter into the inner sanctuary which is the Holy of Holies and worship our Lord God Almighty, and His beloved Son, Jesus Christ, our Blessed Redeemer.

Although worship should be a daily way of life for the

Believer, we must still set aside time to do so with heavenly worship from the Book of Revelation. Worship is natural in heaven, as many continuously bow before our Lord God Almighty, and our Lord and Savior, Jesus Christ. We would gladly take off our crowns of gold, as the twenty-four Elders do. (Revelation 4:10). Then we would cast them before our Lord, while falling down and worshipping Him. We would find it natural and a great honor to give our Lord God Almighty; glory and honor, thanksgiving and power, wisdom, blessing, and might, according to Revelation 7:12.

Similarly, we would find it natural and a great honor to give our Lord and Savior, Jesus Christ, glory and honor, riches and power, wisdom, blessing and strength according to Revelation 5:12. Likewise, we have earthly accounts of saints who worshipped like David, who also entreated us to worship and bow down and to kneel before the Lord our Maker. (Psalm 95:6).

There is also the account of the woman who, in her act of worship, anointed Jesus' head with costly spikenard ointment. (See Matthew 26: 7-13; Mark 14: 3-9). We, like them, should express our praise and worship from deep within our hearts, and they will ascend to God as a sweet-smelling savor. Our Lord is always with us who are saved, for we have His Blessed Holy Spirit dwelling and communicating within us. Therefore, we must not cease to worship our Lord in humbleness of heart and with joy.

MY HEAVENLY WORSHIP FROM THE BOOK OF REVELATION

The way we worship God may vary at different times. Sometimes, I worship our Lord, Jehovah Adonai, with holy worship from the Book of Revelation. Especially, in chapters four and five of the Book of Revelation, God graciously allows us to enter the throne room of heaven and participate in the most divine, awe-inspiring, heavenly worship. Likewise, I worship God saying,

> Dear Lord, we thank You for giving your servant, John, glimpses of heaven while he was banished on the Island of Patmos and living in the most horrific conditions. Additionally, we are grateful that You showed him the perfect rainbow, like an emerald, which is around your majestic throne. Furthermore, out of your throne proceeds lightning, claps of thunder, and voices. We thank You, Lord, for letting John behold You, as You sit on your majestic throne, for to look upon You is as to look at a jasper or sardius stone.

> Dear Lord, we thank You for the seven lamps of fire, burning before your throne, which are the seven spirits of God. We thank You for the twenty-four thrones, which are around your throne. We

thank you for the twenty-four elders who sit on these thrones. They are dressed in their white robes, with crowns of gold on their heads, which they take off and lay before You, and worship You. We thank You, Lord, for the sea of glass, like crystal, which is before your throne. We thank You for the four living creatures, which are round about, in the midst of your throne, having eyes in front, eyes behind, and eyes within their six wings.

We thank You, Lord that the first living creature is like a lion. This living creature represents the kingship of Christ, and brings You praises of all the saints, and of all the wild animals which You created.

We thank You our Lord that the second living creature is like a calf, representing the servitude of Christ. This living creature brings You praises of all the saints, and of all the animals that serve, which You have created.

We thank You for the third living creature, which has a face like a man. This living creature represents the humanity of Christ and brings to You all of the praises from all of mankind whom You have created.

We thank You that the fourth living creature is like a flying eagle, representing the deity of Christ. This living creature brings to You praises of all the saints, and of all the flying, creeping, and swimming creatures which You have created.

The four living creatures rest not day or night,

8

saying:

> Holy, holy, holy, Lord God Almighty, Who was, and is, and is to come!

> Holy, holy, holy, Lord God Almighty, Who was and is, and is to come!

> Holy, holy, holy, Lord God Almighty, Who was, and is, and is to come!

According to Revelation 4:9-11:

Whenever the living creatures give glory and honor and thanks to You, who sits on the throne, who lives forever and ever, the twenty-four elders fall down before You who sits on the throne and worship You who lives forever and ever, and cast their crowns before your throne, saying:

> You are worthy, O Lord,
> To receive glory and honor and power; For You created all things,
> And by your will they exist and were created.

WORSHIP THE LAMB

My Worship continues as:

In Revelation chapter five, John saw in Your right hand, Dear Lord, a scroll sealed with seven seals. This scroll had writings on the inside and the outside. After which, John saw a strong angel proclaiming aloud, "Who is worthy to open the scroll and to loose its seals?" However, there was no one in heaven nor in earth nor under the earth worthy to open the scroll, or to look on it.

Consequently, John wept much for there was no one worthy to open, to read, or even to look on the scroll. Then one of the elders said to John, that he should not weep for behold the Lion of the Tribe of Judah, the Root of David, [Jesus] had prevailed to open the scroll, and to loose its seals. **Jesus alone is worthy**. After which, John beheld and saw, in the midst of the throne, and of the four living creatures, and of the elders, a Lamb standing as if it had been slain. This Lamb, Jesus Christ, had seven horns, and seven eyes, which are the seven spirits of God, which were sent out into all the earth.

Then Jesus (the Lamb who was slain, the only one who was worthy) came and took the scroll out of Your right hand, Dear Lord God Almighty. When the Lamb had taken the scroll, the four living creatures, and the twenty-four elders, fell down before the Lamb. Each of them having a harp, and golden bowls full of incense, which are the prayers of the saints. They sang a new song to Jesus, the Lamb of God, singing:

> You are worthy to take the Scroll, And open its seals; For You were slain, And have redeemed us to God by your blood Out of every tribe and tongue, and people and nation, And have made us kings and priests to our God; And we shall reign on the earth.
>
> Revelation 5:9-10

Truly Lord Jesus, You are worthy, You are worthy, You are worthy. After which, John beheld and heard the unified voice of millions of angels around God's throne, and the voice of the living creatures and of the elders, saying with one loud voice, 'Worthy is the Lamb who was slain to receive power and riches and wisdom, and strength and honor and glory and blessing!' (Revelation 5:12). Here Jesus, the Lamb, receives seven words of complete and perfect worship, they are: glory, honor, *riches*, power, wisdom, blessing, and *strength*. (While His Father, our Lord God Almighty, receives seven words of complete and perfect worship in Revelation 7:12. They are: glory, honor, *thanksgiving*, power, wisdom, blessing, and *might*).

11

To which, John exclaimed that every creature which is in heaven and on the earth and under the earth and such as are in the sea, and all that are in them, he heard say, '...Blessing and honor, and glory, and power, be unto Him (Our Lord God Almighty), who sits upon the throne, and unto the Lamb, (our Lord and Savior Jesus Christ) forever and ever.' (Revelation. 5:13).

As a result, the four living creatures agreed in worship and said, "Amen" or "so be it". In addition, the twenty-four elders fell down in agreement, and worshipped our Lord, who lives forever and ever. (Revelation 5:14). **Amen**.

The seventh angel sounded, and there were great voices in heaven worshipping and saying, "The kingdoms of this world have become the kingdoms of our Lord and of His Christ, and He (our Lord Jesus Christ) shall reign for ever and ever!" (Revelation 11:15). Gloriously, worship in heaven continues, as in like manner, the twenty-four elders, who sit on their thrones before God, fall upon their faces, and worship God.

Thus, saying: "We give You thanks, O Lord God Almighty, The One who is and who was, and who is to come, Because You have taken Your great power and reigned." (Revelation 11:17). Similarly, we too can bow our faces to the ground before the Lord, and say words of adoration, thanks, praise, and worship to Him. We can thank Him for who He is and for what He has done and will do.

In heaven, there is also victorious triumph, as John heard a loud voice in heaven proclaiming:

> Now salvation, and strength, and the kingdom of
> our God, and the power of His Christ have come,
> for the accuser of our brethren (Satan), who
> accused them before our God day and night, has
> been cast down. And they overcame him by the
> blood of the Lamb and by the word of their
> testimony....
>
> Revelation 12:10-11

Subsequently, the everlasting gospel is preached by an angel to those on the earth, asking them to worship our Lord. (Revelation 14:6-7).

Accordingly, in Revelation 14:7, even when the hour of God's judgment had come, there was still admonition to worship our Lord, as the angel states, "Fear God, and give glory to Him...and worship Him who made heaven and earth, the sea and springs of water." This tells us that even when we are going through the most difficult times, we should always remember to keep praising and worshipping our Lord, and His Son, our Lord and Savior, Jesus Christ.

Assuredly, we can say that much of these events from the Book of Revelation have not occurred as yet according to man's calendar. Our time is not as God's time, in which, one day is with the Lord as a thousand years, and a thousand years as a day. (2 Peter 3:8). However, we know that in heaven there is constant, continuous worship. Likewise, on earth, if we do not praise our Lord God Almighty, and our Lord and Savior, Jesus Christ, even the very stones will immediately cry out, Jesus remarked. (Luke 19:37-40).

The pervasiveness and necessity of worship is clearly seen in Revelation 15:2-4, which gives an account of saints who were viciously killed. These martyred saints were slain because they rejected the Antichrist, his image, his mark, and the number of his name. That is, they had gotten the victory over the beast (Antichrist), and over his image, and over his mark, and over the number of his name, by refusing him, and remaining faithful to God. They were standing on a sea of glass, having the harps of God. They were worshipping as they sang the song of Moses, the servant of God, and the song of the Lamb, singing,

> Great and marvelous are Your works, Lord God Almighty! Just and true are Your ways, O King of Saints! Who shall not fear You, O Lord, and glorify Your Name? For You alone are Holy, For all Nations shall come and worship before You, For Your judgments have been manifested.
>
> Revelation 15:2-4

God was well pleased with their worship, and later on we read, that the temple was filled with smoke from the glory of God, and from His power. This was similar to how the temple which Solomon built and dedicated to the Lord was filled with God's glory cloud. Furthermore, the worship of God continues, as John heard the angel of the waters say, "You are righteous, O Lord, The One who is, and who was and who is to be..." (Revelation 16:5). In addition, in Revelation, chapter 16:7 John heard another [Angel] out of the altar say, "Even so, Lord God Almighty, true and righteous are Your judgments."

WORSHIP CONTINUES IN HEAVEN

The worship of our Lord and Savior, Jesus Christ, continues throughout the events in the Book of Revelation. Accordingly, John states in Revelation 17:14, that "...the Lamb will overcome them, for He is Lord of lords, and King of kings; and those who are with Him are called, chosen, and faithful." Whereas, John states in Revelation 19:1-4 that he "...heard a loud voice of a great multitude in heaven, saying, [in worship], "Alleluia! Salvation and glory and honor and power belong to the Lord our God! For true and righteous are His judgments...Again they said, 'Alleluia!'... And the twenty-four elders and the four living creatures fell down and worshiped God who sat on the throne, saying, 'Amen! Alleluia!'"

The praise, adoration, and worship of our Lord continued as John heard a voice coming out of the throne, saying, "...Praise our God, all you His servants and those who fear Him, both small and great!" (Revelation 19:5). John also "...heard, as it were, the voice of a great multitude, as the sound of many waters and as the sound of mighty thunderings, saying, 'Alleluia! For the Lord God omnipotent reigns!' " (Revelation 19:6). These words of adoration, praise and worship can be used as we praise and worship our Lord God Almighty.

Gloriously, in Revelation 19:7-9 worship continues in heaven. During which, Christ's Bride, who is also called the members of Christ's body, all the Believers, or the church, is presented to His

Father for the marriage supper of the Lamb, Jesus Christ. Therefore, "Let us be glad and rejoice and give Him glory, for the marriage of the Lamb has come, and His wife has made herself ready." (Revelation 19:7). John continues in this nineteenth chapter of the Book of Revelation, by saying that to the bride, "... it was granted to be arrayed in fine linen, clean and bright, for the fine linen is the righteousness acts of the saints." (Revelation 19:8). After which, John was instructed to write "Blessed are those who are called to the marriage supper of the Lamb!" (Revelation 19:9).

THE HOLY CITY

We can thank our Lord God Almighty, for showing John, in Revelation chapter 21:1, "…a new heaven and a new earth, for the first heaven and the first earth had passed away. Also, there was no more sea." John also "…saw the holy city, New Jerusalem, coming down out of heaven from God, prepared as a bride adorned for her husband." (Revelation 21:2). John then "…heard a loud voice from heaven saying, 'Behold the tabernacle of God is with men, and He will dwell with them, and they shall be His people. God Himself will be with them and be their God.' " (Revelation 21:3). Additionally, "And God will wipe away every tear from their eyes; there shall be no more death, nor sorrow, nor crying. There shall be no more pain, for the former things have passed away…. Behold, [God] make all things new" (Revelation 21:4-5).

Again, John is instructed to "Write, for these words are true and faithful." (Revelation 21: 5). Further, God proclaims and promises, in verse six through seven of the same chapter, "It is done! I am the Alpha and the Omega, the Beginning and the End…He who overcomes shall inherit all things, and I will be his God and he shall be My son." John also wrote in this chapter, verses ten and eleven, that God carried him away in the spirit, and showed him the great city, the holy Jerusalem, descending out of heaven from God, having the glory of God. This great city's light was like a stone most precious, even like a jasper stone, clear as crystal.

We can continue to give God thanks for this marvelous and glorious city, as is described in Revelation, chapter 21. It has its height, width and length each being about 1,500 miles long. This heavenly city is of pure gold, like clear glass, and the street of the city was of pure gold, like clear glass. It also has a great and high wall, which is made of jasper. The wall of this city has twelve foundations. On these foundations are written the names of Jesus' twelve apostles. The foundations are adorned with all kinds of precious stones. (Revelation 21:16-19).

The first foundation is of jasper, the second is of sapphire, the third is of chalcedony, the fourth is of emerald, the fifth is of sardonyx, the sixth is of sardius, the seventh is of chrysolite, the eighth is of beryl, the ninth is of topaz, the tenth is of chrysoprase, the eleventh is of jacinth and the twelfth of amethyst. (Revelation 21:19-20). The wall has twelve gates, and twelve angels at the gates. These gates have the names of the twelve tribes of the children of Israel written on them. (Revelation 21:12). In this heavenly city, the twelve gates were each of one pearl. (Revelation 21:21).

We must also thank God that there is no need for a temple in the holy city, "...for the Lord God Almighty and the Lamb are its temple." (Revelation 21:22). Furthermore, we thank God that our holy city "had no need of the sun or of the moon to shine in it, for the glory of God illuminated it. The Lamb is its light." (Revelation 21:23). "And the nations of those who are saved shall walk in its light, and the kings of the earth bring their glory and honor into it." (Revelation 21:23-24).

Whereas, in Revelation chapter 22: 1-6, John wrote that he also saw a pure river of water of life, clear as crystal, proceeding from the throne of God and the Lamb. John remarked that "They shall see His face.... There shall be no night there: they need no lamp,

18

nor light of the sun; for the Lord God gives them light. And they shall reign forever and ever." Then, the angel told John that the words he spoke are "faithful and true." (See also Revelation 19:11).

Later on, in Revelation chapter 22:8-9, after John heard and saw those things, he fell down to worship before the feet of the angel who strongly admonished John not to worship him. The angel enlightened John that he (the angel) was John's fellow servant, and of his brethren, the Prophets, and of them who keep the words of this book, who are blessed. The angel also firmly instructed John to "Worship God". (See also Revelation 19:10). This instruction applies to us too. We must worship God! We also thank God for sharing the beauty of the holy city, the New Jerusalem, with us.

As a result, we can truly say, "...Eye has not seen, nor ear heard, Nor have entered into the heart of man The things which God has prepared for those who love Him." (1 Corinthians 2:9). Furthermore, Jesus stated before His crucifixion:

> **Let not your heart be troubled; you believe in God, believe also in Me. In my Father's house are many mansions, If it were not so, I would have told you. I go to prepare a place for you. And if I go and prepare a place for you, I will come again and receive you to Myself; that where I am, there you may be also.**
>
> **John 14:1-3**

Jesus is coming in the clouds of glory to take the righteous to be with Him!

For the Lord Himself will descend from heaven

with a shout, with the voice of an archangel, and with the trumpet of God. And the dead in Christ will rise first. Then we who are alive and remain shall be caught up together with them in the clouds to meet the Lord in the air. And thus we shall always be with the Lord.

1 Thessalonians: 4:16-17

This glorious occasion is called by many, "the rapture", or "the catching away". In which, all the righteous who died from the first man, Adam, to that moment of the 'catching away" or "rapture", will rise first. Many of their bodies may be six feet under the earth or in the sea, but they will arise first. Then all the righteous who are alive at the moment of the "catching away", will rise up to meet them. Our earthly, corruptible, mortal bodies will be changed to heavenly, incorruptible, immortal bodies (1 Corinthians 15:50- 58), and together we will all rise to meet our Lord, Jesus Christ, in the air. What a reunion it will be with righteous loved ones who died before. Gloriously, most of all, what fellowship it will be with our Lord for ever and ever. Oh! That will be glorious, just to see His face will be magnificent, marvelous, and divine.

To which we can say, "Maranatha" or "our Lord comes". This is whom we worship, our Lord God Almighty, and His Son, Jesus Christ, the Lord. Jesus Christ is King of kings and Lord of lords, and is coming soon. Our Lord has prepared the New Jerusalem and many mansions for us. I pray that you will confess Jesus Christ as your risen and glorified Lord and Savior and be caught up to meet Him in "the twinkling of an eye". Thus, we will worship our Lord, with heavenly worship forever and ever, and enjoy all that He has prepared for us.

SOME NAMES FOR OUR LORD

Jesus further affirms in Revelation 22:13, 16, "I am the Alpha and the Omega, the Beginning and the End, the First and the Last I am the Root and the Offspring of David, the Bright and Morning Star." Surely, we can use the names by which our Lord Jesus is referred to, or called, when we worship Him. These names include: the Beginning and the End, the Root and Offspring of David and the Bright and Morning Star. We can definitely say to Jesus, thank you for being my Savior and Lord. You are the Alpha and the Omega, the First and the Last, hallelujah! My Lord, You are the Fairest of Ten Thousands, King of kings and Lord of lords, the Lily of the Valley, the Sweet Rose of Sharon, my Rabbi, my Lord, Jesus Christ.

We can also worship our Lord, as we lovingly and gratefully call Him by other names in the Bible that refer to God as Jehovah (God), Jehovah-Jireh (the Lord will provide), Jehovah-Nissi (The Lord my Banner), Jehovah-Shalom (the Lord sends peace), Jehovah-Rohi (The Lord is my Shepherd), Adonai (Lord, Master), Jehovah-Rapha (The Lord that healeth), and El Elyon (The Most High God). Other names for our Lord Jesus include Jehovah-Tsidkenu (The Lord our Righteousness), Jehovah Hamelech (The Lord, my King), Jehovah-Shammah (The Lord is present), Jehovah Gibbor (The Mighty God; The God who defends), El Kanna (Jealous God), Jehovah Sabaoth (The Lord of Hosts), El Olam (The Everlasting God), Yahweh (God), Emmanuel (God is with us), Wonderful, Counselor, Almighty God, The Everlasting Father, The Prince of Peace, The Son of David, The way, The Truth, and The Life, Messiah, Yeshua, Jewish Messiah, Yeshua Hamashiach (Jesus the Messiah), Majesty, Ancient of Days, The Second Person of the Trinity, and King of Saints. You are the Lamb of God that taketh away the sins of the world.

These are some names for Our Lord Jesus Christ, and as Jesus, our Lord stated, "I and my Father are one." Thus, we can boldly use these and many other names interchangeably for our Heavenly Father or Jesus Christ, our Blessed Redeemer.

Jesus Christ can also lovingly be called by other names that continue to tell what He has done, or will do, for each of us. Furthermore, some of His names tell of His attributes, and what He is to each of us. These names include: my Redeemer, my Heavenly Bridegroom, my Deliverer, my Husband, my Sword and my Shield, my Battle Axe, the Lover of my soul, Majesty on High, my Strong Tower, my Rock, my Fortress, my Surety Divine, my Divine Master, my Conquering King, The Knocker of my heart's door, the Author and Finisher of my faith, my Shield and Defender, my King, my Master, Jesus the name that's above all names, the True Vine, Jesus my Jesus, The Son of the Blessed Lord, Wonderful Savior, The God of my salvation, the Firm Foundation, the Bread of Life, my Song, my Righteousness, my Shield and Buckler, my Joy, The Altogether Lovely One, Awesome God, He who holds the whole world in His hands, my Friend, my Light, and my All in All, my shelter in the time of storm, and the lifter up of my head.

OVERVIEW OF THE BOOK OF REVELATION

This exciting and informative Book of Revelation allows us to witness heavenly worship, and many coming prophetic events. It also primarily reveals who Jesus is, and how He and Our Lord God Almighty are worshipped forever and ever in heaven.

In Revelation 1:8, our Lord and Savior, Jesus Christ begins the Book of Revelation with this powerful assertion. "I am the Alpha and the Omega, the Beginning and the End, says the Lord, 'who is and who was and who is to come, the Almighty.' " The Lord reiterates His powerful claim for emphasis, so that it could not be missed, just three verses later. "I am the Alpha and the Omega, the First and the Last...." (Revelation 1: 11). Further, in verse 17, He restates "I am the First and the Last." (Revelation 1:17).

In like manner, in the second chapter, Our Lord and Savior, Jesus Christ refers to Himself again as, "the First and the Last, who was dead, and came to life". (Revelation 2:8). Likewise, God ends this beautiful book of heavenly worship with the same proclamation in the last two chapters, as He did in the first two chapters. "And He said to me, 'It is done! I am the Alpha and the Omega, the Beginning and the End. I will give of the fountain of the water of life freely to him who thirsts.' " (Revelation 21:6). While again, in the next and final chapter of the Book of Revelation, our Lord and Savior, Jesus Christ culminates this

23

beautiful book by again boldly asserting, "I am the Alpha and the Omega, the Beginning and the End, the First and the Last." (Revelation 22:13). Our Lord and Savior, Jesus Christ says further, "…Surely (not maybe, but surely), I am coming quickly." John exclaims: "Amen. Even so, come, Lord Jesus!" (Revelation 22:20). John ends this powerful Book of Revelation with the Benediction, "The grace of our Lord Jesus Christ be with you all. Amen." This means that the grace or the unmerited favor of our Lord and Savior, Jesus Christ is with us. We do not deserve God's favor, yet He freely gives it to us. Let us also never forget the words of the Angel in Revelation 22:9, "Worship God".

We can also say many of these words of praise, worship, and adoration from this beautiful Book of Revelation, to our Lord God Almighty, and to our Savior, Jesus Christ, as we worship. As a result, God's glorious presence will fill the room or place where we are worshipping, for God inhabits the praises of His children. That is, when we earnestly praise God, He is so pleased with our praise that He comes down from heaven and dwells in our praise.

You see, when we praise and worship God, we are fulfilling His desire for us to worship Him in spirit and in truth. Our Lord commanded us to worship and serve him. Further, Jesus stated in John 4:23-24, "But the hour is coming, and now is, when the true worshippers will worship the Father in spirit and in truth: for the Father is seeking such to worship Him. Truly, 'God is Spirit, and those who worship Him must worship in spirit and truth.'"

In the Book of Revelation, chapters 4,5,7,11 and 19 allow us the privilege of getting glimpses of heavenly worship before and around the throne of our Lord God Almighty, and the Lamb, God's only begotten Son, Jesus Christ. These glimpses of heavenly worship detail the intensity and immensity of the worshipping of:

(1)   millions of the heavenly hosts, (comprising of angels,

24

living creatures, and the elders, who were worshipping God around His throne). (Revelation 5:11). We can gather that millions of angels worship God voluntarily in heaven, as they chose not to join Satan when he warred in heaven against God. (Revelation 12:7-9).

This war occurred, for Satan said in his heart (and got angels to fight with him to try to fulfill his evil intentions), that he would ascend into heaven; he would exalt his throne above the stars of God; he will also sit in the mount of the congregation; he would ascend above the heights of the clouds; and will be like the Most High, who is our Lord, El Elyon, the Most High God. (Isaiah 14:13-14). After being cast out of heaven, to the earth, Satan will no longer be able to go before the Lord in heaven and accuse the "brethren" (i.e., the righteous or saints), as he does now. (Revelation 12:10).

The Apostle John wrote, "Therefore rejoice, O heavens, and you who dwell in them! Woe to the inhabitants of the earth and the sea! For the devil has come down to you, having great wrath, because he knows that he has a short time." (Revelation 12:12). This powerful verse tells us that the devil will be cast onto the earth and can no longer enter heaven to report on Believers in Christ. This will make him very angry, for he will know that he does not have much time left, to do his foul deeds on the earth. This is because Jesus will return shortly thereafter.

Jesus will not be coming as, "Gentle Jesus meek and mild", but as the conquering King of Kings and Lord of Lords. Accordingly, John wrote in Revelation 19:11-16,

> Now I saw heaven opened, and behold, a white horse. And He who sat on him was called Faithful and True, and in righteousness He judges and makes war. His eyes were like a flame of fire, and on His

head were many crowns. He had a name written that no one knew except Himself. He was clothed with a robe dripped in blood, and His name is called The Word of God. And the armies in heaven, clothed in fine linen, white and clean, followed Him on white horses. Now out of His mouth goes a sharp sword, that with it He should strike the nations. And He Himself will rule them with a rod of iron. He Himself treads the winepress of the fierceness and wrath of Almighty God. And He has on His robe and on His thigh a name written:

KING OF KINGS
AND LORD OF LORDS.

This coming to earth of our victorious and triumphant, Lord and Savior, Jesus Christ is referred to as the "second coming of Christ". In the Acts of the Apostles, we read:

And while they looked steadfastly toward heaven as He went up, behold, two men stood by them in white apparel, who also said, 'Men of Galilee, why do you stand gazing up into heaven? This same Jesus, who was taken up from you into heaven, will so come in like manner as you saw Him go into heaven.'

Acts 1:10-11

Jesus Christ will return to earth, as King of kings and Lord of lords.

(2)   The "great multitude which no one can number." (Revelation 7: 9-14). These will be those who come out of the great tribulation. They would have made Jesus Christ their Savior and Lord, and are part of the Bride of Christ.

26

(3) As well as, the martyred saints, who will also be included in the Bride of Christ. (Revelation 15:2- 5).

(4) The voice of a great multitude worshipping. This is the completed Bride of Christ, who is ready for the Marriage Supper of the Lamb. (Revelation 19:6). We all present to Our Lord God Almighty, and the Lamb, Jesus Christ, words of adoration, and glory, for whom the Lord is, was, and will be. This results in continuous worship ringing out in heaven.

The Lord also honored His servant John, by giving him the privilege of enjoying, and sharing, heavenly bliss with us. The Bible tells us that John was the Disciple who leaned on Jesus' bosom at supper. John was also at Jesus' cross with Jesus' Mother, when the other disciples forsook Jesus. In addition, John was banished on the Island of Patmos "...for the word of God, and for the testimony of Jesus Christ." (Revelation 1:9).

John's experience of heaven's worship gives us a lot to look forward to, after we leave this earth. As In heaven, John heard every creature in heaven, earth, under the earth, in the sea, and all that are in each of these places, altogether worshipping the Lord, who sits on the throne, and the Lamb, Jesus Christ. They said in worship, "...Blessing and honor and glory and power Be to Him who sits on the throne, And to the Lamb, forever and ever!" (Revelation 5:13). Most definitely, every person dead or alive will worship God, wherever they will be. It does not matter if they love God or not. They will worship God.

The best gift anyone can receive is the gift of Jesus's free salvation, which He readily offers to us. The Bible states, "For God so loved the world that He gave His only begotten Son, that whoever believes in Him should not perish but have everlasting life." (John 3:16). God loves us so much that He did not just give His only begotten Son to die in our place and pay the price for our sin. Moreover, "...the Son of Man (Jesus Christ) has come to seek and to

27

save that which was lost." (Luke 19:10). The lost is anyone who does not believe and confess the risen Jesus Christ, as Lord and Savior. The Bible also states that "The Lord...is longsuffering towards us, not willing that any should perish but that all should come to repentance." (2 Peter 3:9).

Therefore, remember that the Lord, who created you, loves you, and is seeking you. I beg you to "Seek the Lord while He may be found, Call upon Him while He is near. Let the wicked forsake his way, And the unrighteous man his thoughts; Let him return to the Lord, And He will have mercy on him; And to our God, For He will abundantly pardon." (Isaiah 55: 6-7).

Our Lord loves you and wants to "abundantly pardon" you. Call on Him, and seek Him, for His arms are wide open. He does not impose Himself on anyone. He is waiting on you to accept Him as your Lord and Savior. He wants to save your soul, and give you: hope, peace of mind, forgiveness of sins, healing, blessings, comfort, and make you His child. Please accept the Lord Jesus Christ as your Lord and Savior, and experience being a heavenly worshipper from the Book of Revelation. We can enjoy heavenly worship while we live on this earth, and even more so, when we go to be with the Lord.

HEAVENLY WORSHIP OF THE FOUR LIVING CREATURES

The four living creatures worship God continuously saying:

> **Holy, holy, holy,**
> **Lord God Almighty,**
> **Who was and is and is to come!**

Whenever the living creatures give glory and honor and thanks to Him (our Lord God Almighty) who sits on the throne, who lives forever and ever, the twenty-four elders fall down before Him who sits on the throne and worship Him who lives forever and ever, and cast their crowns before the throne....

Revelation 4:8-10

Then they would worship, exalt, extol and adore Him for creating all things, and for doing so for His pleasure. (See Revelation 4:8-11 KJV). What's more, as this intense and divine worship continues, the four living creatures and the twenty-four elders will fall before the Lamb. Each of them having a harp, and golden bowls full of incense, which are the prayers of the saints. (Revelation 5:8).

In like manner, in Chapter 5:9-10, they sang a new song of worship to Jesus, the Lamb, who was slain but is now alive and victorious. He is the Lion of the Tribe of Judah, the Root of David. Therefore, the four living creatures affirm the worship of the Lamb, our Lord and Savior Jesus Christ according to Revelation 5:14. Thus, again leading to the falling down and worship of the twenty-four elders.

In Isaiah chapter six, the Seraphim are described. They, like the four living creatures of the Book of Revelation have six wings. They veil or cover their faces with two of these wings, because God is so holy, that they are unable to look upon Him. They fly with two of their six wings and veil their feet with their other two wings. (Isaiah 6:2). They protect and also worship God continually saying, **"Holy, holy, holy, is the Lord of hosts; The whole earth is full of His glory!"** (Isaiah 6:3). In like manner, the four living creatures of the Book of Revelation, worship the Lord and say, in Revelation 4:8:" **Holy, holy, holy, Lord God Almighty, Who was, and is, and is to come!"**

Additionally, in Ezekiel chapters one and ten, we read about four living creatures, or Cherubim. They had four faces, four wings, with hands of a man, and legs, with some of their features similar to that of the four Living Creatures of the Book of Revelation. In these and other mentions of living creatures in the Bible, they protect and worship our Lord God Almighty, and the Lamb.

However, before we can worship the Lord, as these heavenly creatures do, firstly, we must be saved. To be saved, we must be born again. This is the most important decision each of us must make. We must each answer the question, what will I do with Jesus? If we do not accept Jesus as our Lord and Savior, one day He will be our judge. Then we would be condemned to an eternity in hell, which is the just recompense or reward for our sinfulness. Therefore, how can we reject Him who loves us so much that He paid the price so that we do not have to go to hell.

Our Lord God Almighty, who created us and loves us, was grieved with mankind's sinful lives. God "...made Him (Jesus Christ) who knew no sin to be sin for us, that we might become the righteous of God in Him." (2 Corinthians 5:21). The Gospel of Luke tells of Jesus' humble birth, in a manger in Bethlehem. During Jesus' ministry, He performed many miracles as turning water into wine, at a wedding in Cana of Galilee; to healing the sick; cleansing the leper; giving sight to the blind; giving hearing to the deaf; and speech to the dumb; making the lame walk; delivering those who had evil spirits; and raising the dead.

Truly, Jesus' "heart is touched with the feelings of our infirmities", and He still heals, delivers, restores to life, and sets free today. Even though, Jesus did so much good, and is God, He was still obedient to His Father, and was willing to be made sin for us. Consequently, God sent His only begotten son, Jesus, to earth, to pay the price for our sins by dying on a sinful, shameful cross. All of Jesus' blood was shed on the cross, to forgive us of all of our sins. A song writer, J. Denham Smith (1817-1889) penned, "all our sins were nailed upon Him, Jesus bore them on the tree (wooden cross). God, who knew them, laid them on Him (Jesus), And, believing, thou art free. Blessed, glorious word, 'forever'! Yea, 'forever' is the word; Nothing can the ransom sever, naught divide them from the Lord."

Jesus said, "...Behold, now is the accepted time; behold, now is the day of salvation." (2 Corinthians 6:2). This means that we can cry out to God to save us right now, and He will. Further, Jesus stated, "Behold, I stand at the door (your heart's door) and knock. If anyone hears My voice and opens the door, I will come in to him and dine (fellowship) with him, and he with Me." (Revelation 3:20). Please ask Jesus to come into your heart, forgive your sins, and make Him your Lord and Savior. If you do, you will be saved from hell, and be made into a new creation. Hence, God's Blessed Holy Spirit will immediately come and dwell within you. Then you can worship the Lord, as the four living creatures do in the Book of Revelation.

THE ABCs OF GOD'S SALVATION PLAN

A- ACKNOWLEDGE/ACCEPT YOUR SINFULNESS

The Psalmist David stated, "Behold, I was shaped in iniquity, and in sin did my mother conceive me." (Psalms 51:5 KJV). Moreover, the Apostle Paul stated in Romans: 3:10, "As is written: There is none righteous, no, not one;" As a result, he later stated in verse 23 of the same chapter of Romans, "for all have sinned and fall short of the glory of God." Romans 5:12 explains "Therefore, just as through one man (Adam) sin entered the world, and death through sin, and thus death spread to all men, because all sinned". This means that when Adam sinned, he plunged the world into sin. As a result, we are all sinners.

It does not matter how many good things or kind acts we have done. We were still conceived in sin. We are unrighteous in God's sight and deserve death (eternal separation from God in hell). Accordingly, in Romans 6:23 we read, "For the wages (pay) of sin is death, but the gift of God is eternal life (with God forever in heaven) in Christ Jesus our Lord." The Apostle John wrote in his first Epistle, chapter 1, verse 8, "If we say that we have no sin, we deceive ourselves, and the truth is not in us." Furthermore, in verse 10 he continues, that if we say that we have not sinned, we make Him (God) a liar, and His (God's) word is not in us. Thus, the first step to salvation is accepting the fact that we are sinners and are unable to save ourselves.

B- BELIEVE THAT JESUS IS LORD AND AROSE
FROM THE DEAD

When we say that Jesus Christ is our Lord, it means that He is the Ruler and Master of our entire lives. He cannot be Lord of only a part of our lives. If He is "not Lord of all, then He is not Lord at all." Further, in Acts 2:36, Luke wrote, as was stated by the Apostle Peter, "Therefore let all the house of Israel know assuredly that God has made this Jesus, whom you crucified both Lord and Christ."

Yes, Jesus is not only Lord of our lives, but God has made Him King of kings and Lord of lords. He is Lord of heaven and earth, with all authority given to Him in heaven and on earth. (Matthew 28:18). He is Lord of all creation and was in the beginning with God and the Blessed Holy Spirit during creation. (Genesis 1:26). Yes, He is omnipresent, omnipotent, and omniscient. He is Lord of all, and He is Christ, The Anointed One, The Messiah.

We also see that in 1 Corinthians 12:3, "...that no one can say that Jesus is Lord except by the Holy Spirit", who would give that revelation. While in 1 Corinthians 6:11 we read, "...But you were washed, but you were sanctified, but you were justified in the name of the Lord Jesus and by the Spirit of our God." Moreover, in Acts 8:16; 19:5, we read that the people were "...baptized in the name of the Lord Jesus."

Also, while Jesus hung on the cross dying, one of the two thieves who was also nailed to a cross next to Jesus, and was also dying, recognized, and believed in Jesus as Lord. He said to Jesus, "Lord, remember me when You come into Your kingdom." (Luke 23:42). Jesus responded to him in love, "Assuredly, I say to you, today you will be with Me in Paradise." (Luke 23:43).

Yes, Jesus is LORD and He arose from the dead. Bearing witness to this, the Apostle Paul wrote, "that if you confess with your mouth the Lord Jesus and believe in your heart that God has raised Him from the dead, you will be saved." (Romans 10:9).

We see that God raised Jesus from the dead as was announced by angels. (Matthew 28:6; Mark 16:6; Luke 24:6). Yes, Jesus arose from the dead (Acts 2:24), and in verse 32 of the same chapter, Luke wrote that they were all witnesses to the same. After Jesus' resurrection, He was first seen by Mary Magdalene (Mark 16:9; John 20:16-17), by the other Mary (Matthew 28:1-10), and by the disciples with whom He fellowshipped. (Mark 16:14; Luke 24:33-43; John 20:19-28, 21:12-15). Jesus was also seen by the men who walked on the road to Emmaus. (Mark 16:12-13; Luke 24:13-31).

Not only was our resurrected Lord, Jesus Christ seen by the women and by His disciples, but He was seen by more than 500 of the Saints at one time. (1 Corinthians 15:6). Jesus was also seen forty days after his resurrection from the dead, as He was taken back into heaven. (Mark 16:19; Luke 24:51; Acts 1:9-11). Yes, in order to be saved, we must believe that Jesus Christ is Lord, and that God raised Him from the dead. Truly, our Lord, Jesus Christ, is alive and is seated at the Father's right hand in glory making intercession for us. (Mark 16:19; Romans 8:34; Hebrews 7:25, 1:3; Isaiah 53:12).

Whereas, Ephesians 2:8-9 states "For by grace you have been saved through faith, and that not of yourselves; it is the gift of God, not of works, lest anyone should boast." The faith through which we are saved is that complete belief, trust, and confidence in Jesus Christ as Lord, who arose from the dead.

C- CONFESS JESUS AS LORD

The thief on the cross confessed Jesus as Lord and was saved from an eternity of separation from God and suffering in hell. Furthermore, at the moment of his death, he was with the Lord in Paradise. As well as, in 1 John 4:15 John wrote, "Whoever confesses that Jesus is the Son of God, God abides in him, and he in God." Most empathetically, Paul wrote:

> [T]hat if you confess with your mouth the Lord Jesus, and believe in your heart that God has raised Him from the dead, you will be saved. For with the heart one believes unto righteousness, and with the mouth confession is made unto salvation. For the Scripture says, 'Whoever believes on Him will not be put to shame'...for the same Lord over all is rich to all who call upon Him. For 'whoever calls on the name of the Lord shall be saved.'
>
> **Romans 10:9-13**

PROCESSES OCCURRING BECAUSE OF SALVATION

Simultaneously, the processes that are occurring because of salvation are:

REDEMPTION

We are redeemed, which means we were bought back from sin and damnation. This is because the precious blood of Jesus was shed for the remission and taking away of our sins. The Apostle Paul wrote that we have redemption through Jesus' blood, even the forgiveness of our sins. (Colossians 1:14). Thus, we are bought with a price, which is Jesus Christ's shameful, sacrificial death on Calvary's cross. Therefore, we are not our own. We belong to our Lord and Savior, who paid the price for us. Accordingly, we are to glorify God in our bodies and souls which are His. Helen Griggs (1951), wrote this chorus, "Gone, gone, gone, gone! Yes my sins are gone! Now my soul is free and in my heart's a song! Buried in the deepest sea, Yes, that's good enough for me! I shall live eternally, Praise God, my sins are gone!" We are redeemed, and now belong to our Lord.

Boldly, our Lord and Savior, Jesus Christ, puts it this way:

37

My sheep hear My voice, and I know them, and they follow Me. And I give them eternal life, and they shall never perish; neither shall anyone snatch them out of My hand. My Father, who has given them to Me, is greater than all; and no one is able to snatch them out of My Father's hand. I and My Father are one.

John 10:27-30

We no longer need the blood of bulls and goats sacrifices to atone for our sins. Jesus Christ, the sacrificial, sinless, spotless, Lamb of God, was separated from His Father, as He bore our sins in His body on the cross. (1 Peter 2:24). As He was in turmoil in the Garden of Gethsemane, He prayed, "O My Father, if it is possible, let this cup pass from Me; nevertheless, not as I will, but as you will." Thus, Jesus became a willing sacrifice, who purchased our souls, when He died in our place on the cross. We have remission of our sins, as Jesus became our sin bearer, and redeemed us from sin. Further, the grave could not hold Him, as He arose from the dead on the third day.

JUSTIFICATION

To be justified means that in God's sight we are made just as if we never sinned. Moreover, the Apostle Paul wrote, "Therefore, having been justified by faith, we have peace with God through our Lord Jesus Christ...Much more then, having now been justified by His blood, we shall be saved from wrath through Him." (Romans 5:1, 9).

All of our sinful deeds were cancelled out, wiped clean, and made right. As a result, where our score card should have a record of all of our sins, the record was wiped out, and we are

38

regarded and treated by God as righteous. Jesus "put our load of sinfulness into the sea of forgetfulness, never to be remembered anymore". The Apostle Paul stated, "Therefore, as through one man's offense (the first Adam) judgment came to all men, resulting in condemnation, even so through one Man's righteous act (the righteous sacrificial death of the second Adam, who is Jesus Christ) the free gift came to all men, resulting in justification of life. For as by one man's (Adam's) disobedience many were made sinners, so also by one Man's (Jesus Christ's) obedience many will be made righteous." (Romans 5:18-19).

Similarly, Luke stated, "Therefore let it be known to you, brethren, that through this Man (Jesus Christ) is preached to you the forgiveness of sins; and by Him everyone who believes is justified from all things from which you could not be justified by the Law of Moses." (Acts 13:38-39).

SANCTIFICATION

We are made a new creation (2 Corinthians 5:17), and are set apart for our Master's use, which is for a sacred purpose. As a result, we can say, "There is therefore now no condemnation to those who are in Christ Jesus, who do not walk according to the flesh, but according to the Spirit." (Romans 8:1). Further, Our Lord God Almighty stated "…Though your sins are like scarlet, they shall be as white as snow; though they are red like crimson, They shall be as wool." (Isaiah 1:18). Therefore, "…we have been sanctified through the offering of the body of Jesus Christ once for all." (Hebrews 10:10). God is a jealous God (Jehovah Kanna), who requires us to serve Him alone.

Moreover, God sanctifies us, and sets us apart for His use, even while things are not going well for us. Like Jonah in the belly of the fish; like Joseph in the pit, slavery, jail, and

39

Potiphar's house; like Daniel in the lion's den; like David while running from Saul; like Paul and Silas in prison; and like the Apostle John banished on the Island of Patmos, we are set apart, and God will use what we glean in our adversity for His glory. God will get the glory out of our lives, and will reward us for what we endure for His Name's sake.

GLORIFICATION

Romans 8:30 states, "Moreover whom He (our Lord God Almighty) predestined, these He also called; whom He called, these He also justified; and whom He justified, these He also glorified." Surely, we who are saved are already glorified, elevated, and ennobled as children of the King, as we are raised up in newness of life. Additionally, we will be further glorified, as Christ's Bride, when He presents us to our Almighty God. Most definitely, our Heavenly Bridegroom, Jesus Christ, will present us to His Father as His Bride, for whom He died. We, Christ's Bride will be "without spot, wrinkle or blemish", and will be glorified in heaven, at the Marriage Supper of the Lamb. Further, we will continuously be glorified, and give glory, in the presence of our Lord for all eternity.

However, while on this earth, the road we have to travel as children of God is not easy. Yet marvelously, the Apostle Paul wrote, "...that the sufferings of this present time are not worthy to be compared with the glory which shall be revealed in us." (Romans 8:18).

GOD SAVED A WRETCH LIKE ME

I can say like the Apostle Paul, **"...sinners, of whom I am chief...."** Yet, in spite of my numerous sins, God who knew the end from the beginning; God who knew every bad thing that I would ever do, still loves me. He took me into His loving arms, saved me, and made me His child. It does not matter what you have done, if you got into drugs, fornication (voluntary sexual intercourse with someone you are not married to), lying, cyber bullying, pornography, or any other sin. You are like the lost sheep whom Jesus, the good Shepherd, would go out and search for until He finds you. Our Lord is taking the time to seek and save those who are lost. You might have wasted or misused your inheritance, the gifts and talents which God gave to you.

Further, like the Prodigal son, you might have lived a life with shame, sin, and selfishness. So did many of us who are saved. Be courageous Beloved, it's not too late. Come out of that sin which so easily afflicts you. "For what shall it profit a man if he gains the whole world and loses his own soul?" Please, look to Jesus now and live. Go to our Blessed Redeemer, Jesus Christ. He has already taken your place on Calvary.

As the Prophet Isaiah wrote of our Lord and Savior, Jesus Christ, many hundreds of years before His scourging and crucifixion, "But He was wounded for our transgressions, He was bruised for our iniquities; The chastisement for our peace was upon Him, And by His stripes we are healed." (Isaiah 53:5).

41

While Isaiah 52:14 also stated that "...His visage was marred more than any man, and His form more than the sons of men."

This powerful and prophetic picture of Christ's suffering and sacrificial death for us, depicts Our Lord and Savior, Jesus Christ as our eternal and final sacrifice. This is because of God's grace, or His undeserved and unmerited favor to us. Therefore, like the Prodigal son, stop being willing to eat hogs' slop. Instead, go to your Father, and tell Him that you have sinned against Him, and ask Jesus to save you. Most definitely, the Bible says that "... whoever calls on the name of the Lord shall be saved...." Romans 10:13. Surely, "...now is the accepted time; behold, now is the day of salvation." (2 Corinthians 6:2).

Jesus Christ... "loved us, and washed us from our sins in His own blood, and has made us kings and priests to His God and Father. To Him be glory and dominion forever and ever. Amen." (Revelation 1:5-6). Accordingly, overcomers will reign with Christ. Jesus Christ bears this out in Revelation 2:26-28, when He said, "And he who overcomes, and keeps My works until the end, to him I will give power over the nations...'and I will give him the morning star.' " In verse ten of the same chapter it states that martyrs for Christ will also be given a crown of life. While in Revelation 2:17 it further states that overcomers will be given of the hidden manna to eat. They will also be given a white stone with a new name written, which only the overcomer will know.

"WHAT WILL YOU DO WITH JESUS?"

"Neutral you cannot be". If you do nothing, you have already rejected Jesus, and condemned your soul to an eternal hell. Remember what David said refers to us too. "Behold, I was brought forth in iniquity, and in sin my mother conceived me." (Psalm 51:5). Therefore, if you do not ask Jesus to forgive you of your sins, and to save you, your name would not be found written in the Lamb's Book of Life. You also will be condemned to an eternity in hell, as you stand before God at the Great White Throne Judgment. (Revelation 20:11-15). "He who believes in the Son has everlasting life; and he who does not believe the Son shall not see life, but the wrath of God abides on him." (John 3: 36). Jesus has all power over hell, death, sin and the grave.

Accept Jesus as your Savior now, for those whose names are not found written in the Lamb's Book of Life, will perish and suffer forever in the Lake of Fire. (Revelation 20:12-15). Where there will be wailing and gnashing of teeth. (Matthew 13:37-42, 49-50). Where the fire is not quenched, and the worms do not die. (Mark 9:43-48).

"For what will it profit a man if he gains the whole world and loses his own soul?" (Mark 8:36). Earthly riches are for a season. No one can take their earthly wealth with them into eternity. Nor can anyone use earthly wealth to purchase privileges in hell, or to buy a way out of hell. There is no partying in hell, as everyone is individually suffering forever and ever. Hell is a place of outer darkness, in which there is "weeping, wailing, and gnashing of teeth".

There are no rights in hell. Satan is not the god or a leader in hell. It is a place of extreme torment, where Satan too will be tormented. Accordingly, the Disciple John wrote, "The devil, who deceived them, was cast into the lake of fire and brimstone where the beast (the Anti-Christ) and the false prophet are. And they will be tormented day and night forever and ever." (Revelation 20:10) Thus, they who look upon Satan will say, "Is this **the man** who made the earth tremble, Who shook kingdoms…?" (Isaiah 14:12-16).

Tomorrow is not promised to anyone. Today, like the Prodigal son, return home to your Father. Confess your sins to Him, and ask Him to forgive your sins. Then confess Jesus as your Lord. He will save you from the wrath to come, and will make you His child. To be saved or born again, you can call upon the Lord in your own words, from deep within your heart, or you can say this simple prayer, if you mean it.

PRAYER OF SALVATION

Dear Heavenly Father, I confess that I am a sinner. I repent of my sins. I confess with my mouth that Jesus Christ is Lord. I believe in my heart that He died on the cross, and You raised Him from the dead. I believe that Jesus is the only way to You, and I accept Jesus as my Lord and Savior. Father forgive my sins, save me and make me your child. Thank You Lord for saving me.

TO GROW AS A CHRISTIAN

YOU NEED TO READ THE WORD OF GOD (THE HOLY BIBLE)

To grow spiritually, you need to feed on the Word of God daily. That is, you need to read and learn from God's Holy Word, the Holy Bible daily. After accepting Jesus Christ as your Lord and Savior, you are considered a newborn baby in Christ. The Apostle Peter wrote that you, "as newborn babes, desire the pure milk of the word, that you may grow thereby." (1 Peter 2:2).

Therefore, as a new believer in Christ, you are likened unto a newborn baby, which needs milk (the Word of God) to grow successfully. Just as a newborn baby needs milk daily to grow, you need to read the Word of God (the Holy Bible) daily to grow and become stronger in the Word. You can read from any part of the Holy Bible. Some Christians suggest that the Gospel of John, in the New Testament is a good place for new believers to start reading, and learning about our Lord and Savior, Jesus Christ. However, please read the whole Bible if possible, from the Book of Genesis through the Book of Revelation, as it all tells about our Lord, and Savior, Jesus Christ.

YOU NEED TO TALK TO GOD IN PRAYER

We can freely talk to God in prayer. At the moment that Jesus said on the cross "It is finished", and died, He had taken our sins upon Himself, and paid the price for our sins, once and forever. At that moment, "...the veil of the temple was torn in two from top to bottom". (Matthew 27:51; Mark 15:38). As a result, we have direct access into God's presence. This means that we can go boldly into the presence of our Lord in prayer. We can be assured that prayer moves God. (James 5:17-18; 1Kings 17-18). We can also look at Paul and Silas in prison, as is recorded in Acts 16:23-34. They were put in the inner prison for security, and their feet were restrained with chains.

However, at midnight, they were praying and singing hymns, when suddenly there was a great and strong earthquake. This earthquake was so powerful that it shook the foundations of the prison. All of the prisoners' chains fell off, and the prison doors swung wide open. This demonstrated the power of unified prayer and praise, and led to the prison guard, and his whole household, accepting Jesus Christ as their Savior and Lord, and being baptized.

Prayer is essential for the Believer in Christ. God answers prayer and says in His Word, "Ask, and it shall be given to you.... For everyone who asks receives...." (Matthew 7:7-8). Further, James 4:2 states"...you do not have because you do not ask." Prayer can take the form of giving God thanks, praise, glory, adoration, worship, intercession, making requests to God, or just talking to God, and pouring our hearts out to Him. It can also be the declaring and decreeing of God's promises to us, and of the rights and privileges He gave us, as kings and priests with Christ, who are "Children of the Kingdom". We need to talk to God in prayer.

Additionally, Luke wrote, "but we will give ourselves continually to prayer and to the ministry of the Word." (Acts 6:4). Whereas, Luke wrote also that our Lord, Jesus Christ spoke a parable to them espousing, "...that men always ought to pray, and not lose heart (or faint)...." (Luke 18:1). Further, James encouraged us in his Epistle, to "Confess your trespasses to one another, and pray for one another, that you may be healed. The effective, fervent prayer of a righteous (that's who you now are when you are saved) man avails much." (James 5:16).

Whereas, the Apostle Paul penned, "I desire therefore that the men pray everywhere, lifting up holy hands, **without wrath and doubting**." (1 Timothy 2:8). Talk to God, in your heart, or audibly, or in a quiet place, or wherever you are. Talk to God as you would talk to a friend, for God is a friend who sticks with us closer than a brother.

YOU NEED TO ASSEMBLE YOURSELF TOGETHER WITH OTHER BELIEVERS AND GROW FROM THE MINISTRY OF GOD'S WORD

In Acts 6:4, Luke wrote, "But we will give ourselves continually to prayer, and to the ministry of the word." Not only must you read your Bible and pray, you must also join and consistently fellowship with other believers in Jesus Christ, where the Word of God is ministered. Furthermore, the Apostle Paul penned, "Not forsaking the assembling of ourselves together, as is the manner of some, but exhorting one another, so much the more, as you see the Day (of Christ's return) approaching." (Hebrews 10:25).

Thus, we are to fellowship in a church or gathering of Believers which preaches that Jesus, who was God incarnate (in the flesh), is Lord. Further, that Jesus is the "only begotten Son" of God, who was born of the Blessed Virgin Mary. (Luke 1:48, 42). In addition, that Jesus loved us so much that He died on the cross to save us from sin. God raised Jesus from the dead on the third day. As well as, that our Lord and Savior, Jesus Christ is coming back to take us (Believers in Jesus Christ), to be with Him.

YOU NEED TO PRAISE AND WORSHIP THE LORD, FOR HE INHABITS OUR PRAISES

The prophetic Book of Revelation demonstrates to us how we should, and would worship our Lord God Almighty, and His son, our Lord and Savior, Jesus Christ. We also find praises to our Lord in the Psalms. In which, David, who God declared was a man after His own heart (1 Samuel 13:14; Acts 13:22), wrote, "O Lord, our Lord, how excellent is Your name in all the earth, Who have set Your glory above the heavens! ...O Lord, our Lord, How excellent is Your name in all the earth!'' (Psalm 8:1, 9).

Further, in Psalm 9:1-2 David wrote, "I will praise You, O Lord, with my whole heart; I will tell of all Your marvelous works. I will be glad and rejoice in You; I will sing praise to Your name, O Most High." In Psalm 34:1-3, David wrote, "I will bless the Lord at all times; His praise shall continually be in my mouth. My soul shall make its boast in the Lord; The humble shall hear of it and be glad. Oh, magnify the Lord with me, And let us exalt His name together." Additionally, we read, "As the deer pants for the water brooks, so pants my soul for You, O God." (Psalm 42:1).

Plus, Psalm 100:1-4 states, "Make a joyful shout to the Lord, all ye lands! Serve the Lord with gladness; Come before His presence with singing. Know that the Lord, He is God; It is He who made us, and not we ourselves Enter into His gates with thanksgiving,

And into His courts with praise. Be thankful to Him, and bless His name." While in Psalm 103:1-4 David instructs, "Bless the Lord, O my soul; And all that is within me, bless His holy name! Bless the Lord, O my soul, And forget not all His benefits: Who forgives all your iniquities, Who heals all your diseases, Who redeems your life from destruction, Who crowns you with lovingkindness and tender mercies."

Furthermore, in verses 20-22 of the same Psalm, David stated, "Bless the Lord, you His angels, Who excel in strength, who do His word, Heeding the voice of His word. Bless the Lord, all you His hosts, You ministers of His, who do His pleasure. Bless the Lord, all His works, In all places of His dominion. Bless the Lord, O my soul!" In addition, Psalm 104:1-2 begins with, "Bless the Lord, O my soul! O Lord my God, You are very great: You are clothed with honor and majesty, Who cover Yourself with light as with a garment, Who stretch out the heavens like a curtain."

Whereas, David stated in Psalm 145: 1-7, "I will extol You, my God, O King; And I will bless Your name forever and ever. Every day I will bless You, And I will praise Your name forever and ever. Great is the Lord, and greatly to be praised; And His greatness is unsearchable. One generation shall praise Your works to another, And shall declare Your mighty acts. I will meditate on the glorious splendor of Your majesty, And on Your wondrous works. Men shall speak of the might of Your awesome acts, And I will declare Your greatness. They shall utter the memory of Your great goodness. And shall sing of Your righteousness."

Additionally, Psalm 146:1-2 states, "PRAISE the LORD! Praise the Lord, O my soul! While I live I will praise the Lord; I will sing praises to my God while I have my being." This Psalm ends with a resounding, "Praise the Lord!" Psalm 147:1 also begins with "PRAISE the LORD!" After which, the Psalmist David continues, "For it is good to sing praises to our God; For it is pleasant, and praise is beautiful." This Psalm also ends with the urgency to "Praise the Lord!" While, Psalm 148:1 also begins with "PRAISE the LORD!" This Psalm commands that our Lord is to be praised from the heavens, in the heights, to in the depths, which includes hell.

In this Psalm, God is to be, and will be praised by all of His creations, including: his angels, the sun, moon, stars, heavens, serpents, and from everything, even great sea creatures. God is to be praised by: fire, hail, snow and vapor; stormy wind fulfilling God's word; mountains, and all hills, fruitful trees and all cedars; beasts, and all cattle; creeping things, and flying fowls; kings of the earth, young men, young women, old men, and children, all are to, and will, as the Psalm ends, **"Praise the Lord!"**

Psalm 149:1 also begins with, "PRAISE the LORD!" Then it continues, "Sing to the LORD a new song, And His praise in the assembly of the saints." This Psalm also ends with "Praise the

Lord!"

Further, Psalm 150 culminates with "PRAISE the LORD! Praise God in His sanctuary; Praise Him in His mighty firmament! Praise Him for His mighty acts; Praise Him according to His excellent greatest! Praise Him with the sound of the trumpet; Praise Him with the lute and harp! Praise Him with the timbrel and dance; Praise Him with stringed instruments and flutes! Praise Him with loud cymbals! Praise Him with clashing cymbals. Let everything that has breath praise the LORD." The inspirational Book of Psalms magnificently ends with the previously stated command to "Praise the LORD!" Consequently, whosoever offers God praise glorifies God! (Psalm 50:23).

THE GREAT COMMISSION

You must go and make disciples! In the Gospel according to Mark, Jesus' last and great commission to His disciples before He was received up into heaven was, "Go into all the world, and preach the gospel to every [person]." (Mark 16:15). Likewise, Matthew tells of this great commission as Jesus exhorts His disciples, "Go therefore, and make disciples of all nations, baptizing them in the name of the Father, and of the Son, and of the Holy Spirit, teaching them to observe all things that I have commanded you; and lo, I am with you always, even to the end of the age." (Matthew 28:19).

Before we go on any long journey, we leave final important instructions for our children, or for whoever we leave in charge. In like manner, Jesus thought of His final commission as important. Therefore, commanding His disciples, which includes, we who are saved, to go into all the world and teach His wonderful Gospel of salvation, which is in Him (Jesus Christ) only. Accordingly, Jesus commissioned, "...you shall be witnesses to Me in Jerusalem, and in all Judea and Samaria, and to the end of the earth." (Acts 1:8). Go and preach the Gospel of Jesus Christ! While doing so, always remember that the God of Abraham, Isaac and Jacob, Elohim, is with you. He will empower you for the journey.

AN URGENT CALL TO WORSHIP

Revelation 14:6-7 states,

"Then I saw another angel flying in the midst of heaven, having the everlasting gospel to preach to those who dwell on the earth-to every nation, tribe, tongue, and people-saying with a loud voice, 'Fear God and give glory to Him, for the hour of His judgment has come; and worship Him who made heaven and earth, the sea and springs of water.'"

If we are warned of a soon coming disaster, we would attend to what is most important to keep us safe. An example of this is, if we are warned that we are in the path of an approaching tornado, we would desperately try to get out of its path, or seek shelter in a room that is underground. We can glean from the Scripture reading (Revelation 14:6-7) that even at the hour of judgment, God, who created man, loves mankind greatly. His deep love was evident in Him sending His angel to beg all of mankind to come away from their sinful way of living, and obey God, to avoid impending doom of their souls.

What did the angel ask mankind to do to avoid this doom? (1) Fear God, which means to have godly respect and reverence for God, regarding Him as their Lord; (2) give glory to God; (3) and worship God who made heaven, and earth, the sea and springs of water.

God's doom is imminent, and God gives mankind the most

important things to do to avoid definite danger and condemnation of their souls. After they reverence God as Lord, they are to engage in giving Him glory. This is a form of worship, honor, thanksgiving, and adoration, and they are to worship God, the Creator.

God did not tell them that after they have reverenced Him as Lord, they are to pray for things, or preach, or go about their usual business. Even though, these things are all very important for us to do. Yet, at the hour of God's judgement, God is sending His angel to beg them to reverence Him as Lord. Then they are to give Him glory and worship Him. They are to do this just as they are, and with their possible limited Christian experience, and for the limited time they have left on this earth.

God wants them to just reverence, glorify and worship Him who created all things, right at that time, and just as they are. They are to worship the Lord in humbleness of heart. Worship is therefore most important for the Believer, as it is for God's good pleasure. It is worship that God deserves and desires from us on earth; even if, we have just accepted Jesus Christ, as our Lord and Savior. It is worship that God deserves, and also requires from us right before we go to heaven. It is also worship that God deserves and receives in heaven.

We may argue that this may not be the hour of God's judgment. We may say or believe that we have much time left on this earth. Only God knows. Even if Jesus Christ does not come this week or this month, time is not our own. Moreover, we do not know the day or hour of Christ's return in glory, only the Father knows. (Matthew 24:36; Mark 13:32).

We may also reason and say, that people have been looking for the Messiah's (Christ's) return from even before the time of the disciples. We may add, that He has not returned as yet. We may think that we have plenty time before His coming, to store

55

up wealth and enjoy sinful pleasures. Then when we get old, we will accept Jesus Christ as Lord. However, we could pass on from this life to eternity at any time, even tonight. (Luke 12: 16-21). We still have to be ready to meet our God, right now, at this time.

Our Lord has made many of His children watchmen for this season. (Ezekiel 3:17-21; 33:1-20). We are to urge all to accept the risen and glorified Lord, Jesus Christ, as Savior and Lord. Certainly, as His return in the clouds of glory is drawing near. Then, please begin worshipping our Lord God Almighty, and His Son, Jesus Christ, the Lamb of God, "in spirit and in truth". This is the time for true heavenly worship. In addition, God lovingly gave us examples of heavenly worship in the Book of Revelation, which we can follow.

When we become saved, our Lord God Almighty, El Shaddai, will refine us, and will made us anew. Thus, enabling us to **worship our Lord in the beauty of holiness**. We were created to worship, and we shall worship our Lord God Almighty and His Son, our Lord and Savior, Jesus Christ throughout eternity.

Jesus clearly stated, that this is the time (hour) "...when the true worshippers will worship the Father in Spirit and truth, for the Father is seeking such to worship Him." (John 4:23). God created us and He is seeking us to worship Him in Spirit and truth, at this time. (See John 4:23-24, Psalm 113:1-3, 146:1-2, 145, 100, 150).

You may then ask, why does the devil keep trying to stop you from worshipping your Lord? You may also wonder why he makes you feel unworthy, by reminding you of bad things which you did in the past? The answer can be found in the Gospel of Matthew 4:1-11. Here we read about the three temptations of our Lord and Savior, Jesus Christ, by the enemy, the devil, who is also called Satan, great dragon, serpent of old (see Revelation 12:9), and "... Lucifer, son of the morning!" (Isaiah 14:12).

After the devil tempted Jesus the second time, Jesus boldly said to the devil, "It is written again. You shall not tempt the Lord your God". This clearly states that Jesus rebuked the devil by telling him that he, the devil, should not tempt the Lord Jesus, who is the devil's God. Therefore, Jesus, proclaimed His deity, and was unchallenged by the devil, when Jesus told the devil that he (the devil), should not tempt "the Lord, who is Jesus, and is the devil's God. Subsequently, the devil tried the third time to tempt Jesus, but this time, the devil showed his true intention, which was to steal Jesus' worship and position of worship.

This was evidenced when the devil told Jesus that he will give Jesus all the kingdoms of the world and their glory, if Jesus will fall down and worship him, the devil. Jesus knew that all the kingdoms of the world and all their glory were already His, and boldly and emphatically told the devil to get away from Him.

Jesus again cited the Word of God, by telling the devil, "For it is written" that the devil is the one who shall worship Jesus, the Lord, the devil's God, and that the devil should serve Jesus only. The devil was unable to dispute Jesus' proclamation of lordship over him. Nor could the devil dispute Jesus' words to the devil that he, the devil, should serve only Jesus, his Lord and God, as "it is written".

The creation, the devil, tried to get the Creator, God, to worship the creation. We can look at Genesis 1:26 in which God said "Let Us make man in Our image, according to Our likeness...." Here the words "Us" and "Our" are referring to God, the Father; God the Son, Jesus Christ; and God the Holy Spirit, all three in one. We can look further at John 1:1-3, in which the Apostle John wrote, under inspiration of the Holy Spirit, "In the beginning was the Word (who is Jesus Christ), and the Word was with God, and the Word was God. He was in the beginning with God. All things were made through Him (Jesus Christ), and without Him nothing was made that was made." Thus, Jesus Christ is also God, the Creator, and is to be worshipped and served by Satan, and all creation.

As a result of these truths, the devil's only option was to flee from Jesus' presence. That's what makes the devil flee from us too, so we can worship our Lord God Almighty, and His only begotten Son, our Lord and Savior, Jesus Christ. The devil could not steal Jesus' worship, or position, which is what the devil implicitly asked of Jesus, when he asked Jesus, to fall down and worship him, the devil. We are also assured of the devil's future worship of our Lord and Savior, Jesus Christ, in Philippians 2:10-11. In this passage we read, "that at the name of Jesus every knee should bow, of those in heaven, and those on earth, and of those under the earth (which includes the devil, for that's where the devil will be cast according to Revelation 20:10), and that every tongue should confess that Jesus Christ is Lord, to the glory of God the Father." (See also Isaiah 45:23).

Worship is the most desired commodity, which belongs to God only. However, the Bible states in the Epistle of James 4:7, that if you resist the devil, he will flee from you. Whenever situations and troubles come to stop the worship of your Lord, say applicable verses from the Bible that relate to the situation, back to the devil. You can tell him of what God delivered you from, and that you trust God to do it again, i.e. the word of your testimony. Always remember to remind him that Jesus' blood covers you from all sin. (See Revelation 12:11).

It is also important to pray the Lord's Prayer, in which we ask God not to lead us into temptation. (Matthew 6:9-13; Luke

11:2-4). We should also learn Bible verses, so we could say as the Psalmist David, "Your word I have hidden in my heart, that I might not sin against You. (Psalm 119:11). Truly, God's "...word is a lamp to [our] feet And a light to [our] path." (Psalm 119:105). If we hide God's word in our hearts; then, when the tempter comes, we can draw from the memorized word. These proclamations will defeat the enemy, and have him flee from us.

Many have questioned God over the centuries, about His creation, man, His positioning of man, and the abundant care He showers on man. Even Job, and the Psalmist David did the same. (See Job 7:17-18; Psalm 8:4-8, 144:3-4; Hebrews 2:6-9). However, the Bible states that God created such to worship Him. Other Scriptures state that God created us for His glory (Isaiah 43:7). Yet Revelation 4:11 (KJV) states that God created us for His pleasure. Do we have other purposes for our lives while we are alive? Yes, we do. Some of these can involve our gifts and callings. Yet, we can be assured that God loves us, and created us for His glory, good pleasure, and to worship Him, for "such a time as this".

Moreover, from the Book of Revelation, we see the purpose and prevalence of continuous heavenly worship. This is before and around the throne of our Lord God Almighty, and of the Lamb, our Lord and Savior, Jesus Christ. This worship is for our Lord's good pleasure. Thus, the time is now, when we should become true worshippers. As such, we should worship our God with Heavenly worship from the Book of Revelation, which includes glory and praise, as we worship. Again, I plead with everyone who has accepted Jesus Christ as Lord and Savior, to begin worshipping. Yes, please worship our Heavenly Father, and our Lord and Savior, Jesus Christ, and commune with God's Holy Spirit, who is dwelling within you. How beautiful it is to be a part of a whole church congregation's unified worship of

59

our Lord. The atmosphere is charged, as God sits there and inhabits the congregation's praise. We are also changed.

Our Blessed Holy Spirit, and Jesus Christ, our Lord, intercede to God on our behalf. Our Blessed Holy Spirit also teaches us, speaks to us, convicts us of sin, directs us, and fills us with dunamis power from above. Therefore, do not grieve the Holy Spirit by living sinful lives, or do not quench the Holy Spirit by not responding to given corrections or convictions. Some may ask, as I am now saved, and God has forgiven my sin, can I continue to live a sinful life? The Apostle Paul emphatically stated, "...Shall we continue in sin that grace may abound? Certainly not!" (Romans 6:1-2). Besides, "...we (who are saved) shall all stand before the judgment seat of Christ (the Bema)....So then each of us shall give account of himself to God." (Romans 14:10-12).

God's Blessed Holy Spirit can change the hard, cold, unforgiving, and unrepentant soul into a "purpose driven" worshipper. This can surely occur after that person believes in Jesus as Lord, and confesses Jesus, our risen and glorified Lord, as Savior and Lord. Then by earnestly giving thanks, praises, and glory to God, while worshipping our Lord, that garment of heaviness will be replaced with a tender heart of praise and worship.

The Christian journey is not "an easy road". There are struggles, challenges, trials, and good times. However, we can be confident that our awesome and omnipotent Lord God Almighty is always with us. As we journey along the Christian pathway, God leads us through the hills and valleys of life. (See Psalm 23; 91). Our Lord also gives us an internal sweet peace in the middle of any storm, as He already suffered for our peace. (Isaiah 53:5; John 14:27; Phil 4:7). Our Lord God Almighty does not only loves us, forgives our sins and saves us. He also keeps us, beautifies us and prospers us. Moreover, God has blessed, and is blessing us. Truly, as we praise and worship the Lord, He showers us with abundant blessings.

HOW WAS JESUS WORSHIPPED?

Our Lord, Jesus Christ, was worshipped in different ways by different people:

(1) "...[T]hey saw the young Child with Mary His mother, and **fell down and worshipped Him**. And when they had opened their treasures, they presented gifts to Him: gold, frankincense, and myrrh."

Matthew 2:11

(2) Jesus' disciples worshipped Him aloud and said, "Blessed is the King who comes in the Name of the LORD! (See Psalm 118:26). Peace in heaven and glory in the highest!"

Luke 19:37-40

(3) In addition, we read: "And behold a leper came and **worshiped Him, saying,** 'Lord, if You are willing, You can make me clean.'"

Matthew 8:2

(4) Sometime after, "...behold, a ruler came and **worshiped Him, saying,** 'My daughter has just died, but come and lay Your hand on her and she will live.'"

Matthew 9:18

(5) Jesus was also worshipped, as He triumphantly entered Jerusalem, and a huge crowd cheered Him on. They spread their clothing and branches for the colt to walk on. They waved palm branches and said in worship,

> Hosanna!   Psalm 118:26
> Blessed is He who comes in the name of the LORD!
> Blessed is the Kingdom of our father David
> That comes in the name of the Lord!
> Hosanna in the highest!
>   Mark 11:1-10
>   SEE ALSO Matthew 21-1-11; Luke
>   19:28-38; John 12:12-13

Different forms of worship of our Lord:

We read that, "...the whole multitude of the disciples began to rejoice and praise God with **a loud voice** for all the mighty works they had seen, saying: 'Blessed is the King who comes in the name of the Lord! ' " (Luke 19:37-38). This declaration told that Jesus was King, and that He was sent by God, and had all rights, honor and authority of the Lord.

While similar to the angel and multitude of heavenly host who announced Jesus' birth, (Luke 2:14), the disciples boldly continued in worship by saying, "Peace in heaven and glory in the highest." (Luke 19:38). Hence, the disciples loudly praised and worshipped our Lord, Jesus Christ, with words of adoration and honor. In a similar manner, our Lord and Savior, Jesus Christ, the Lamb, was also loudly worshipped by the twenty-four elders, four living creatures, and millions of angels as they said with **"a loud voice"**:

Worthy is the Lamb who was slain
To receive power and riches and wisdom,
And strength and honor and glory and blessing!
                                    Revelation 5:12

In Luke 19:38, we see where our Lord, Jesus Christ, was also worshipped through quoted Scripture, which praised and testified of Him. This was done by His disciples, when they quoted Psalm 118:26, as did the large crowd when He rode triumphantly into Jerusalem on a colt. (Mark 11:9; Zechariah 9:9).

Our Lord, Jesus Christ was further worshipped through the singing of hymns and songs that testified of Him. This is demonstrated in Revelation 5:9-10. In these verses, the four living creatures and the twenty-four elders sang a new song of praise and worship to the Lamb, Jesus Christ, our Lord and Savior. Likewise, did the martyred saints of Revelation 15:2-5. Additionally, the Psalmist David encourages us to joyfully sing praises aloud to our Lord, even from our beds. (Psalm 149:5; 146:1-2; 147:1, 7; 149:1).

The leper of Matthew 8:2 worshipped our Lord Jesus Christ by calling Him "Lord". Then alike the ruler of Matthew 9:18, they demonstrated the faith they had in Jesus Christ, as a form of worship. The leper's faith was apparent when he said that Jesus could heal him from leprosy. Whereas, the ruler showed his faith in our Lord, when he said, that his daughter had died. However, he believed that if Jesus laid His hand on her, that she would come back alive. This was called worship by God. Even though, we do not know what their postures were at that time. The Scriptures tell us they "worshiped Him saying". Therefore, just confessing Jesus as Lord; and expressing faith in His power to perform miracles for us; as we make our request known unto

64

Jesus, our Lord, is worship.

Accordingly, one of the thieves who was crucified on the cross next to Jesus went to heaven, (Paradise), right after worshipping our Lord, in spirit and in truth. The thief's act of worship was similar to that of the leper of Matthew 8:2. He, alike the leper, acknowledged and confessed Jesus Christ as Lord, and made a request of Jesus, which only God could fulfill. Then, the dying thief asked Jesus, "Lord, remember me when You come into Your kingdom". This dying man had the faith and belief that his Lord, Jesus Christ, would not stay dead. Indeed, he had the faith that his Lord would come into His kingdom and show him mercy. This is a form of worship alike that of the leper of Matthew 8:2, and the ruler of Matthew 9:18. (See also Matthew 15:21-28).

These forms of worship required faith or "complete trust" in God. Hebrews 11:1 states "Now faith is the substance of things hoped for, the evidence of things not seen." Furthermore, verse six of this chapter of faith tells us, "But without faith it is impossible to please Him, for he who comes to God must believe that He is, and that He is a rewarder of those who diligently seek Him."

Worship can also be performed through an act. Jesus was worshipped as a baby by the wise men from the East. "[T]hey saw the young Child with Mary His mother, and fell down and worshiped Him...." (Matthew 2:11). They brought him gifts of gold (signifying His Kingship), frankincense (signifying His Priesthood), and myrrh (signifying His death).

Further, the woman who anointed our Lord's head, with costly fragrant spikenard ointment, did so as an act of worship. This act prepared our Lord for His burial. (Matthew 26:6-13; Mark 14:3-9). Another act of worship was the worship of the enthusiastic crowd as Jesus triumphantly entered Jerusalem. We are also instructed to lift up hands in the sanctuary and bless the Lord. (Psalm 134:2; 1 Timothy

2:8). The Psalmist David also encouraged us to play instruments aloud in praise of our Lord. (Psalm 150; 149:3). Besides, David danced intensely before the Lord, (2 Samuel 6:14- 16), and encouraged us to praise the name of the Lord, with dance. (Psalm 149:3).

As a result, we can say that our Lord and Savior, Jesus Christ was worshipped in different ways. Some of these were: with words of praise and adoration; with the quotation of Scripture, which tells of Him; through the singing of hymns and songs which testify about Him; and through acknowledging and confessing Him as Lord, and making a request to Him. The request was made while having the faith that He is God, and can perform it. Worship of our Lord was also through the pouring out of acts of deep love and special sacrificial giving (costly spikenard ointment). Equally, we can use any and all of these forms of worship as we honor, adore, glorify, and praise our Lord, in the beauty of holiness.

HOW WORSHIP WORKS

Worship is as a woman boldly and proudly telling her husband: how strong he is; how he makes her feel safe as he holds her in his powerful arms; how much he means to her; that he is her shield and defender; and how she cannot live without him. At such a moment of rhapsody, if an attacker comes to attack the wife, the husband will knock him out. How dare anyone or anything intrudes on her worship of her lord, or tries to attack the worshipper! Worship which is our act of glory, adoration, honor and reverence to God, also provides a secret weapon against the attacks of the enemy and his devices. Remember God, our protector, is with us and inhabits our praises. His angels will also chase the enemy, and conquer whatever the enemy sends to attack us.

Then, shackles are broken, just as when Paul and Silas prayed and sang hymns to God at midnight, while incarcerated. Other entrapments as sickness, poverty, lack, infirmities, and oppressions are broken off of us. God freely gives us His healing, deliverance, provisions, protection and wholeness. Accordingly, when God comes down and inhabits our praise, simultaneously, broken things are made whole.

Never forget to whisper, say in your heart, and say or sing loud praises to our Lord. Do not be afraid or ashamed to lay prostrate at His feet. Besides, you can worship; in a similar manner, in which you would bow and worship an earthly king or queen. Or bow before one who has your destiny in his hands. You can also kneel, or fall down (or drop on your knees, with your face bowing towards the ground) in worship, as the four living creatures, and the twenty-four elders do in heaven, according to the Book of Revelation.

You do not only have to wait until you get to heaven to do so. You can worship God with heavenly worship while you are on earth. After all, it is our Lord who knew us, even before we were shaped in our mother's womb. It is our Lord God Almighty who fashioned us in the womb. Therefore, we must worship Him with a heart full of gratitude. We are true worshippers, and God created "such" to worship Him.

We may ask, where can I worship God? You may worship the Lord: while you are laying in your bed; while kneeling in your home; while sitting on a chair; while incarcerated in prison as Paul and Silas; while in pain in a hospital bed, and calling out to Jehovah Rapha, your healer; while jogging or walking; while driving in your car; while fellowshipping in church; while performing your daily duties; while dancing before the Lord with all your might as David did; while suffering as John did on the Island of Patmos, being ostracized from civilization, friends and family; or quietly in your prayer closet. It is our great and awesome God who gives us breath and the ability to live, move, and to be whole. (Acts 17:28)

Let us express our love for our Lord by worshipping Him, for He is worthy of worship and praise. Let us love and worship our Lord for giving us a way back to Himself, through Jesus' sacrifice for us at Calvary. Let us love and worship our risen and glorified Lord, Jesus Christ. Let us fill the earth with the worship of our Lord God Almighty,

and His Son, our Lord and Savior, Jesus Christ.

The worship of our Lord should pour out from broken, desperate, tender, obedient, and loving hearts. Our worship should flow out of our pain, distress, and love. Even though, our marriage, children, relationships, health, finances, and employment may be in trouble, this is when we should worship our Lord more. Worship is not about us. It's all about Him.

Therefore, in the midst of trouble, we must worship our "…Lord God Almighty, The One who is and who was and who is to come." (Revelation 11:17). Remember, that His heart is touched with the feelings of our infirmities. (Hebrews 4:15 KJV). Yes, worship moves God!

As we worship our Lord, our pains decrease, and our focus on our Lord increases. God is a present help in the time of trouble. (Psalm 46). Worship Him and let the outpouring of our worship saturate our world. Let it impact the world and our brokenness for the better. Let the whole earth be "full of His glory". Thus, let us, the true worshipper, do as the angel reminded John, and "Worship God!" Accordingly, let us do so, with "Heavenly Worship from the Book of Revelation"!

www.ingramcontent.com/pod-product-compliance
Lightning Source LLC
LaVergne TN
LVHW051154080426
835508LV00021B/2626